Robert Blackwell

**Original Acrostics, on Some of the States and Presidents of the United States**

And Various Other Subjects, Religious, Political and Personal

Robert Blackwell

**Original Acrostics, on Some of the States and Presidents of the United States**
*And Various Other Subjects, Religious, Political and Personal*

ISBN/EAN: 9783337234331

Printed in Europe, USA, Canada, Australia, Japan

Cover: Foto ©ninafisch / pixelio.de

More available books at **www.hansebooks.com**

# Original Acrostics,

ON SOME OF THE

## STATES AND PRESIDENTS

OF THE

## UNITED STATES,

And Various Other Subjects,

## RELIGIOUS, POLITICAL AND PERSONAL.

ILLUSTRATED

## With Fifty Engravings.

---

By ROBERT BLACKWELL.

---

NEW YORK:
PUBLISHED FOR THE AUTHOR.
1871.

# INDEX.

| | |
|---|---|
| Arkansas | 72 |
| Adams, John Quincy | 19 |
| Atlanta | 80 |
| Acklin, Mrs. Col. | 35 |
| Applewhite, Dr. J. N. | 84 |
| Augusta | 50 |
| Blackwell, Robert | 5 |
| Brown, Gov. | 13 |
| Brandy | 24 |
| Bell, William | 34 |
| Buchanan, James | 37 |
| Bell, John | 45 |
| Bourland, Ellen F. | 47 |
| Blackwell, Elizabeth | 88 |
| Bell, B. S. | 47 |
| Blackwell, John L. | 57 |
| Blackwell, Mary T. | 89 |
| Bragg, Laura J. | 66 |
| Bible | 63 |
| Blackwell, Micajah | 100 |
| Baldwin, R. | 105 |
| Cheatham, Dr. W. N. | 25 |
| Crenshaw, Annie E. | 23 |
| Cole, Dr. Isaac N. | 41 |
| Childs, S. R. | 44 |
| Cars | 46 |
| Clay, Henry | 49 |
| Cable, Atlantic | 55 |
| Columbus, Christopher | 59 |
| Carolina, North | 60 |
| Connecticut, | 101 |
| Charity—Faith—Hope | 107 |
| Cosgrove, Charles | 85 |
| Chase, The | 67 |
| California | 72 |
| Croge, Spencer | 73 |
| Comet | 76 |
| Cole, Dr. J. L. | 76 |
| Canton, Ladies of | 77 |
| Douglas, Stephen A. | 78 |
| Dameron, E. H. | 64 |
| Dean, Elizabeth | 97 |
| Dippers, Snuff | 92 |
| Delaware | 83 |
| Emmet, Robert | 108 |
| Earth | 34 |
| Fox, Maggie C. | 42 |
| Flushing | 101 |
| Fillmore, Millard | 99 |
| Fame | 80 |
| Grant, Ulysses | 31 |
| Gospel, go ye | 103 |
| Georgia | 72 |
| Hendrickson, Hendrick A. | 12 |
| Hill, Frances E. | 21 |
| Hope | 42 |
| Hume, Mr. | 56 |
| Head, River | 82 |
| Hill, Nettie | 95 |
| Hampshire, New | 69 |
| Howard, Ann | 95 |
| Jefferson, Thomas | 14 |
| Johnson, Andrew | 17 |
| Jesus | 39 |
| John | 40 |
| Jackson, Ladies of | 53 |
| Jennings, Sallie E. | 54 |
| Jamaica | 82 |
| Jerusalem | 89 |
| Jackson, Andrew | 9 |
| Lincoln, Abraham | 29 |
| Lafayette, M. De | 38 |
| Lancaster | 43 |
| Light | 76 |
| Machine, Sewing | 35 |
| Mist | 41 |
| Mary | 44 |
| Maryland | 51 |
| Marriage | 52 |
| Moon, Sarah P. | 54 |
| Moon, Wm. T. | 56 |
| McLean, Judge | 11 |
| Massachusetts | 11 |
| North, Soldiers of | 105 |
| North, Ladies of | 104 |
| News | 40 |
| North Carolina | 60 |
| Nebraska | 63 |
| Oil, Ambrosial | 46 |
| Oddities, Two | 58 |
| Pennsylvania | 102 |
| Polk, James K. | 23 |
| Prince, Mistress M. | 60 |
| Rum | 24 |
| Rush | 51 |
| Revelries | 65 |
| Reves, Nancy | 62 |
| S. T. Mary | 66 |
| Selfish, The | 64 |
| Smith, Fanny | 62 |
| Springfield, Ladies of | 94 |
| Springs, Chalybeate | 86 |
| Sleep, Amount of | 85 |
| Sun | 70 |
| Stars | 67 |
| Sherman, Gen. | 79 |
| Terry, Susan A. | 24 |
| Thomas, M. H. | 45 |
| T. Miss Harriet | 96 |
| Tea | 50 |
| Tennessee | 60 |
| Thomas, Emma | 73 |
| Taylor, Zachery | 75 |
| Titsworth, Sarah A. | 70 |
| Union | 5 |
| Utah | 77 |
| Vermont | 83 |
| Webster, Daniel | 81 |
| Washington, City of | 68 |
| Wife, My | 91 |
| Washington, George | 7 |
| York, New | 102 |

ROBERT BLACKWELL'S

## ACROSTIC.

Rhyming is now my occupation,
Oft times I write on subjects new,
By this I rise to observation,
Expecting pay for what I do;
Regarding men of higher station,
They read my book, and pay me, too.

Burlesque me not, ye wise and knowing,
Let me but work and make my rhymes,
All I would ask is half a showing,
Come, gentlemen, hand o'er your dimes;
Keep them no more in pockets tight,
When people work they want their pay.
Encourage worth with talents bright—
Little critics, now clear the way,
Learn first to spell before you write.

## ACROSTIC.

United in heart, to thee firmly we cling;
Not fearing the world while thy praises we sing;
Impressed with thy charms, thy grandeur and might,
Our pride and our glory, while to thee we hold tight,
No nation can awe us or put us to flight!

ROBERT BLACKWELL'S

## ACROSTIC.

Go, read the history of the earth,
Each book, and try to find
One man so loved for sterling worth,
Respected, more refined—
Greater, and of a better birth,
Endeared more to mankind.

We read, that ere to fight he went,
All brave of heart to do and dare,
Some one beheld our hero bent,
His God to seek in humble prayer.
In that behold his faith in God—
Not in the prowess of his sword.
Great chieftain, gift of heaven above,
There never was a man
On earth deserved more praise or love,
Not e'en since time began.

**First President of the United States.**

Born in Virginia, February 22, 1732.  President from 1789 to 1797—eight years.  Died December 1, 1799.

---

### *MORAL LESSON—WASHINGTON'S FILIAL PIETY.*

GEORGE WASHINGTON, when young, was about to go to sea as a midshipman; every thing was arranged; the vessel lay opposite his father's house; the little boat had come on shore to take him off, and his whole heart was bent on going. After his trunk had been carried down to the boat, he went to bid his mother farewell, and saw the tears bursting from her eyes. However, he said nothing to her; but he saw that his mother would be distressed if he went, and, perhaps, never be happy again. He just turned round to the servant, and said, "Go and tell them to fetch my trunk. I will not go away to break my mother's heart." His mother was struck with the decision, and she said to him, "George, God has promised to bless the children that honor their parents, and I believe that he will bless you." The young man who thus honored his parents was afterward honored by his countrymen, and will be to the end of time.

## ACROSTIC.

Great and noble, brave and free,
Ever faithful, kind was he;
No one could bend his iron will,
Earth could not his spirit quell;
Read his exploits o'er and o'er,
And you'll love him more and more.
Low though he sleeps, his virtues shine,
And will until the end of time.
Now go with him through all life's scenes,
Down to the battle of New Orleans;
Respect the course he is pursuing,
Enter on the battle's plain,
Witness the dying and the slain;
Judge from what you see him doing,
All his efforts were not in vain;
Cities though are saved from ruin,
Kindled is the very air—
See the British in despair—
On each foe destruction hurl'd—
Now his fame surrounds the world.

**Seventh President of the United States.**

Born in North Carolina, March 15, 1767. President from 1829 to 1837—eight years. Died June 8, 1845.

---

### *MORAL LESSON.*

Lord Tenterden, who was the son of a barber, had too much good sense to feel any false shame on that account. It is related of him, that when, in an early period of his professional career, a brother barrister, with whom he happened to have a quarrel, had the bad taste to twit him on his origin, his manly and severe reply was, "Yes, sir, I am the son of a barber; if you had been the son of a barber, you would have been a barber yourself."

## ACROSTIC.

Just read his dear name, and his merits proclaim;
Unflinching from duty, he rose up to fame;
Discerning true worth in the Christians of earth,
God giving him faith, he sought the new birth.
Embracing which, he exulting could see
Jehovah's own Son his Savior to be.

Made glorious and bright, with heaven in sight,
Captivating our hearts, he marched on to might.
Leaving nothing undone, while 'neath the bright sun,
Ever faithful and kind, many victories he won;
And with his last words, he shouted in death;
Not fearing to die, surrendered his breath.

## ACROSTIC.

Make all thy men in this Union confide,
And resolve to sustain it, since thousands have died,
Suffering with hunger, with hardships, and pains,
Sickness, and tortures, to free us from chains;
And since those chains that bound us once fast
Can never more gall, while the Union shall last,
Hold back the turbulent and make them see
Union of States is the strength of the free;
So should thy sons in the future be found
Endeavoring to scatter dissension around;
Those traitors arrest, though fierce and though bold,
Their crimes to punish before we are sold
Slaves to Europe, that tyrant of old.

One of the original thirteen. Population 1860, 1,231,494. Number of square miles, 7,800.

## ACROSTIC.

Hating all wrong, let us be strong,
Each holy joy to saints belong;
Now, knowing this, the Lord of might
Direct our feet in ways of right;
Rich and the poor, the low and the high,
In the cold grave must shortly lie;
Convinced of this, now let us pray,
King Jesus take our sins away,

And make us both more useful be.

How swift our lives away they flee;
Exposed to pain at every breath,
Now let us both prepare for death.
Don't let us care what sinners say;
Remember, if we humbly pray,
Immanuel God, without a doubt,
Converting us, will make us shout;
Kept by free grace, the Christian knows
Salvation's streams still saving flows.
Oh, let us, then, in Christ confide,
Nor fear to own for us he died.

## ACROSTIC.

Glittering fame
Of pearly white,
Vigorous, and
Ethereal bright,
Reflect his worth.
Now on him gaze,
Our people's choice,
Resolve to praise.

Just view him now,
On glory bent,
Striving to make
Each one content;
Proclaiming truth,
His name should be

Extolled by all,

Both bond and free.
Receiving praise,
O'er earth he goes,
With head above
Nefarious foes.

---

## ACROSTIC.

Made under the law, defiled by sin,
And by the spirit pure within;
Redeemed by blood, from sin set free,
Your soul will live while ages flee.

## ACROSTIC.

THREATENED by foes on land and sea,
HEEDING not the powers that be,
OUR fathers, struggling to be free,
MADE us renowned, by giving thee
A pen to write a declaration,
SCORNING chains and degradation,

JUST in time to save a nation,
EXPRESSING worth by demonstration;
FLINCHING not, with pen in hand,
FOR us so boldly took thy stand,
ELEVATED by command,
ROLLED the ink to save our land.
SO long as stars and stripes shall wave
O'ER this land of the *fair and brave*,
NATIONS will respect thy grave.

**Third President of the United States.**

Born in Virginia, April 13, 1743. President from 1801 to 1809—eight years. Died July 4, 1826.

---

*MORAL LESSON.—WISDOM LEARNED FROM NATURE.*

AN Italian bishop struggled through great difficulties without repining or betraying the least impatience. One of his intimate friends, who highly admired the virtues which he thought it impossible to imitate, one day asked the prelate if he could communicate the secret of being always easy. "Yes," replied the old man, "I can teach you my secret with great facility; it consists in nothing more than making a right use of my eyes." His friend begged of him to explain himself. "Most willingly," returned the bishop. "In whatever state I am, I first of all look up to heaven, and remember that my principal business here is to get there; I then look down upon the earth, and call to mind how small a place I shall occupy in it, when I die and am buried; I then look abroad into the world, and observe what multitudes there are who are in all respects more unhappy than myself. Thus I learn where true happiness is placed—where all our cares must end, and what little reason I have to repine or complain."

## ACROSTIC.

All o'er these States, from sea to sea,
Ne'er did we feel more need of light;
Depending on Jehovah, we
Regard thee, sir, as clothed with might;
Each praying God to give to thee
Wisdom to guide our people right.

Justly, O then, thy power extend,
Opposing wrong of every kind!
Hold to the right, each State defend,
North and the South together bind.
Secession rose but had an end,
Overpowered as was designed,
No more an advocate to find.

**Seventeenth President of the United States.**

Born in North Carolina, December 29, 1808. Succeeded to the Presidency on the assassination of President A. Lincoln, April 14, 1865.

## ACROSTIC.

Noted afar as the city of rocks,
And heroes brave and ladies fair,
She sits enthroned on her cliff, and mocks
Her envious rivals everywhere.
View all her noble works of art—
Increasing. Wealth on every hand;
Lawyers, Statesmen, schools, and mart;
Little to blame and much to praise,
E'en here, if rich, would I spend my days.

## ACROSTIC.

People of this and distant climes
Regarded him as one of worth;
Each knowing him, did him adore,
So long as he remained on earth.
In learning none could him excel,
Discussion was to him delight;
Exploring was his mind, but still
Ne'er was he known to swerve from right.
Think of the height to which he rose,

Jeweled with fame's bright diadem;
Of those he was surrounded by
He stood above the best of them.
Now if you wish to blot his name

Quite from beneath the sky,
Uplift the sea first from its bed,
Its mighty waves defy;
Not only so, but make the stars
Cease, at your word, to run,
Yon silver moon, too, pluck it down,

And paralyze the sun;
Do all which we have named above,
And then you can, no doubt,
Make men forget his useful life,
Sweep, too, his memory out.

**Sixth President of the United States.**
Born in Massachusetts, July 11, 1767. President from 1825 to 1829—four years. Died February 23, 1848.

---

### MORAL LESSON.—CICERO.

The great Roman orator was one day sneered at by one of his opponents, a mean man of noble lineage, on account of his low parentage. "You are the *first* of your line," said the railer. "And you," replied Cicero, "are the *last* of yours."

## ACROSTIC.

First, wisdom seek, and with the meek
Rejoice, the name of Christ to speak;
And 'neath the sun, all errors shun,
Nor in the way of sinners run;
Child as thou art, Christ wants thy heart,
Entreats thee, too, from sin to part;
So let us bow to Jesus now,

Embracing faith, he tells thee how
Vile sinners may find out the way,
And keep the road to endless day.

His wondrous love be thine to prove;
In Christ we live, in him we move;
Low at his feet, that safe retreat,
Let us his matchless worth repeat.

---

*MORAL LESSON.*

Lord Tenterden, who was the son of a barber, had too much good sense to feel any false shame on that account. It is related of him, that when, in an early period of his professional career, a brother barrister, with whom he happened to have a quarrel, had the bad taste to twit him on his origin, his manly and severe reply was, "Yes, sir, I am the son of a barber; if you had been the son of a barber you would have been a barber yourself."

ROBERT BLACKWELL'S

## ACROSTIC.

Justice and truth he loved from his youth,
And, as in years, he grew old,
More wise he became, till he won a proud name,
Ever to be bright; while stars give us light,
Shall the world of his wisdom be told.

Kindest of men, there ne'er was a pen

Pointed with gems could praise him too high;
O'er the statesman true now hundreds we view,
Lamenting the hour when God, by his power,
Kindled disease, and caused him to die.

**Eleventh President of the United States.**

Born in North Carolina, November 2, 1795. President from 1845 to 1849—four years. Died June 15, 1849. Glory to his name and peace to his ashes.

---

His fame it will last while ages go past,
Kind husband, great statesman, though dead,
Our people do boast of his valor and trust,
On the marble which covers his head.

(*Inscribed to Mrs. James K. Polk.*)

---

### MORAL LESSON—KNOCKING AWAY THE PROPS.

"See, father," said a lad who was walking with his father, "they are knocking away the props from under the bridge. What are they doing that for? Won't the bridge fall?"

"They are knocking them away," said the father, "that the timbers may rest more firmly upon the stone piers which are now finished."

### THE APPLICATION.

God often takes away our earthly props, that we may rest more firmly on him. God sometimes takes away a man's health that he may rest upon Him for his daily bread. Before his health failed, though, perhaps, he repeated daily the words, "Give us this day our daily bread," he looked to his own industry for that which he asked of God. That prop being taken away, he rested wholly on God's bounty. When he receives his bread, he receives it as the gift of God. God takes away our friends, that we may look to him for sympathy. When our affections were exercised on objects around us, when we rejoiced in their abundant sympathy, we did not feel the use of Divine sympathy; but when they were taken away we felt our need of God's sympathy and support. We were brought to realize that he alone can give support, and form an adequate portion for the soul. Thus are our earthly props removed, that we may rest firmly and wholly upon God.

## ACROSTIC.

Red fire of hell—uncooling drink,
Unpitying foe, now stop and think;
Make men no more to ruin sink.

---

There is a sufficient quantity of fermented and distilled liquor used in the United States to fill a canal 14 feet wide and 120 miles long.

The liquor saloons and hotels of New York city, if placed in opposite rows, would make a street—like Broadway—eleven miles in length. If the victims of the rum traffic were there also, we should see a suicide at every mile, and a thousand funerals every day. Such are its appalling results!

---

## ACROSTIC.

Blasting hopes of man and wife,
Real source of grief and strife;
A curse on land, a curse on sea,
No man of sense will drink of thee,
Drying all the vitals up,
Yet fools this poison daily sup.

## ACROSTIC.

Denouncer of wrong and defender of right,
Occupying a place resplendently bright;
Commanding our songs, our homage, and our praise;
Though having strong vision, on thee when we gaze,
Our eyes are dazzled, for we see so much light
Reflected from thee that we scarcely can write.

We wish thee much pleasure through all coming days,

And thy most charming bride, deserving our praise,

Convinced of her merits, her graces, and worth,
Having wed her, the best of mortals on earth,
Extol her, protect her, each day through the year,
And, others forsaking, her presence prefer;
'Twill give her true joy thy affection to tell,
Her face wreathed with smiles, all confusion to quell,
And drive away darkness, preventing all strife,
Making thousands adore both thee and thy wife.

## TAKE WARNING.

The judgment-day is just ahead,
And ere one hundred years be fled,
All those now living will be dead,
And sleeping in their narrow bed.

Then let us all from slumber wake,
And this resolve with firmness make:
We will at once our sins forsake,
And the bright road to glory take.

## ACROSTIC.

More fool than wise, more knave than saint,
And yet he had so many charms,
Reclining on his chair of ease,
The people took him to their arms;
In all his glory they saw him rise,
Not clothed with virtue, but with disguise

Vows he broke from day to day,
And though he made a great display,
No good of him can mortal say.

But still from us he homage claims,
Unmindful of his traitorous aims;
Robed in the garments of a foe,
Enticing men with him to go—
Not to heaven, but down below.

**Eighth President of the United States.**

Born in New York, December 5, 1782. President from 1837 to 1841—four years.

---

### FABLE—THE FOX AND THE GOAT.

A Fox having tumbled by chance into a well, had been casting about a long while to no purpose how he should get out again, when, at last, a goat came to the place, and wanting a drink, asked Reynard whether the water was good. "Good," says he; "aye, so sweet that I am afraid I have surfeited myself, I have drank so abundantly." The goat, upon this, without any more ado, leaped in, and the fox, taking advantage of his horns, by the assistance of them, as nimbly leaped out, leaving the poor goat at the bottom of the well to shift for himself.

### THE APPLICATION.

The doctrine taught us by this fable is no more than this: that we ought to consider who it is that advises us before we follow the advice. For, however plausible the counsel may seem, if the person that gives it is a crafty knave, we may be assured that he intends to serve himself in it more than us, if not to erect something to his own advantage out of our ruin.

The little, poor country attorney, ready to starve, and sunk to the lowest depths of poverty, for want of employment, by such arts as these, draws the 'squire, his neighbor, into the gulf of the law; until, laying hold on the branches of his revenue, he lifts himself out of obscurity, and leaves the other immured in the bottom of a mortgage.

## ACROSTIC.

Perceive him now standing before us to-day,
Resemblance of all that is noble and true;
Enamored at the sight, though he sleeps in the clay,
Still we love from our hearts his image to view.
In his converse and presence we all took delight;
Discerning true wisdom in Freedom's great son;
Endowed with good sense, he rose up to might,
Ne'er swerving from duty, ere his race it was run—
The rebels and traitors he put them to flight.

All knew him as honest, persevering, and good;

Long services like his will ne'er be forgot,
It was at the head of our councils he stood,
Not dreaming of danger, when, alas! he was shot.
Could grieving awake our Statesman and guide,
Our weeping and wailing would do it we know;
Loving his country, like a martyr, he died,
Not knowing the man who laid him so low.

**Sixteenth President of the United States.**
Born in Hardin Co., Ky., February 12, 1809. President from 1861 to his assassination, which took place April 14, 1865.

---

## ACROSTIC.

Dreadful monster—ruthless foe!
Ever traveling to and fro,
And causing tears of grief to flow;
The great and loved, and those that be
Hale and strong, must yield to thee.

## ACROSTIC.

Give him due praise
Each man that be
Now living on
Earth's soil free,
Read how he fought,
And bravely, too,
Leading his men.

Great, wise, and true,
Reflecting worth;
A hero, he
Ne'er will succumb
To foes that be.

ULYSSES SIMPSON GRANT was born in Clermont County, Ohio, on the 27th day of April, 1822, in a small one-story cottage, which is still standing on the banks of the Ohio, commanding a view of the Ohio River and the Kentucky shore.

---

## MORAL LESSON—LUTHER MARTIN AND THE YOUNG LAWYER.

We heard an anecdote of this distinguished lawyer, a few days ago, which we remember to have met with in print, but which is so good that it will do to tell again.

Martin was on one occasion riding to Annapolis in a stage coach, in which was a solitary companion, a young lawyer, just commencing the practice of law. After some familiar conversation, the young gentleman said:

"Sir, you have been remarkably successful in your profession—few have gained so many cases—will you be good enough to communicate to me, a beginner, the secret of your wondrous success?"

"I'll do it, young man, on one condition, and that is, that you defray my expenses during my stay of a few days at Annapolis."

"Willingly," replied the young man, hoping thereby to profit greatly by the communication.

"The secret of my success," said Martin, "may be discovered in this advice, which I now give you, namely: '*Deny every thing, and insist upon proof.*'"

On reaching Annapolis, Luther Martin was not very self-denying in the enjoyment presented by a fine hotel; the substantials and general refreshments were dispatched in a manner quite gratifying to mine host. The time for return at length came. The young man and Martin stood together at the bar, demanding their respective bills.

Martin's was enormous, but on glancing at it, he quietly handed it to the young lawyer, who, running his eye over it, leisurely returned it with the utmost gravity.

"Don't you intend to pay it?" said Martin.

"Pay what?" said the young lawyer.

"Why, pay this bill. Did you not promise, on the route downward, that you would defray my expenses at the hotel?"

"My dear sir," said the young gentleman, "I deny every thing, and insist upon proof."

Martin at once saw that he was caught, and eyeing his young friend a moment or two, he said, pleasantly, "You don't need any counsel from me, young man—you don't need any counsel from me."

This fine machine,
Before us seen,
While we its charms proclaim;
We only know
That it can sew,
But cannot tell its name.
Still we suppose
'Twas made by those
Who understood the art
Of forming right,
Machin'ry bright,
To cheer each loving heart.
'Tis making dimes
More prized than rhymes;
Earth with its fame is ringing.
While sitting there,
That lady fair
About its worth is singing.

## ACROSTIC.

Sweet is the breath of morn when we arise;
Unspeakably sweet to look upon
So wondrous a work as the lucid skies;
And a creature formed like thee, bright one,
No living man can fail to prize.

Aurora gilds the morn with light—

'Tis her's to drive all gloom away,
Each one behold her charms and might,
Resplendent goddess of the day,
Round earth she drives her chariot bright,
Yet not of her, of thee, we write.

---

## ACROSTIC.

Annie, sweet Annie, it ne'er was my lot
'Neath the blue bending skies, in palace or cot,
'Neath the tropical sun or the snow-covered crest,
In the Orient East, or the beauty-famed West,
E'er to meet, e'en in dreams, with an angelic face,

Enshrined in a form that an houri would grace;

Combined in one being, virtue, gentleness, love,
Refining the circle in which she might move,
Enhancing, exhalting, enriching with good,
Ne'er till now in such presence enrapt have I stood.
Still long have I hoped such a lady to meet—
Have fondly believed such a being I'd greet;
And now, having found her, I fain at thy shrine
Would kneel, worship, idolize, beauty like thine.

## ACROSTIC.

Exploring all its beauties, I never can its Author doubt,
As fancy flies from pole to pole, and the eye looks round about,
Reflecting on its wondrous size, remembering all I see,
The blessed Lord from nothing spake; and for a worm like me
He left his shining home above, and died upon a tree.

---

## ACROSTIC.

With firmness and with holy fear,
In the work of Christ engage,
Let nothing ever thee deter,
Loud although the tempest rage,
In deep retirement God is nigh,
And in the gloom of night
Man may on his grace rely,

Benignity, truth and might;
Ever, then, adore his name,
Let sinners scoff, the world defame,
Let heaven be thy only aim.

*(Of Virginia.)*

## ACROSTIC.

Men sing of thy graces, and drink to thy health,
Renowned for thy beauty, thy wisdom, and wealth,
Scarce know we one mortal so good as thyself.

Could we be permitted thy worth to proclaim,
Our hills and our valleys would ring with thy name,
Loud sounding, like thunder, extending thy fame,

And waking from slumber all mortals around,
Completely enchanting the learned and profound;
Knowing thy merits, thy praises would sound;
Loving most justly such perfection to view,
Interesting our hearts, with equals but few,
Ne'er swerving, while living, thy pleasures pursue.

---

## ACROSTIC.

My niece most kind, for bliss designed,
As one of sense, improve thy mind;
Respecting, too, each mortal true,
Yield not to sin, like others do.

Eschewing wrong, be firm and strong,

Craving knowledge, now march along,
And gladly sing, to Christ I cling,
Maker of earth and every thing.
Proud would I be thy face to see,
Because thou art so dear to me;
Each hour, each day, for thee I pray.
Loving the right, with death in sight,
Let us for realms of glory fight.
    (*Of Crawford Co., Arkansas.*)

## ACROSTIC.

Juggling old men we hate to see,
And such a man should never be
Made for to rule the brave and free.
Evil-minded, most greedy, too,
See how he spends the revenue.

Base-hearted, mean, intriguing, sly,
Unfit to live, unfit to die,
Corrupted by a Northern band,
Hating the South our native land—
A curse to all, to child and sire—
No one should such a fame desire.
All the prayers of this whole nation
Need now be made for his salvation.

(*Composed just before he left the White House*, 1861.)

---

*MORAL LESSON—THE SLANDERER'S FALL.*

One of the favorites of Artaxerxes, ambitious of getting a place possessed by one of the king's best officers, endeavored to make the king suspect that officer's fidelity; and to that end, sent information to court full of calumnies against him, persuading himself that the king, from the great credit he had with his majesty, would believe the thing upon his bare word, without further examination. Such is the general character of calumniators. The officer was imprisoned; but he desired of the king, before he was condemned, that his cause might be heard, and his accusers ordered to produce their evidence against him. The king did so; and as there was no proof of his guilt but the letters which his enemy had written against him, he was cleared, and his innocence fully confirmed by the three commissioners who sat upon his trial. All the king's indignation fell upon the perfidious accuser, who had thus attempted to abuse the confidence and favor of his royal master.

## ACROSTIC.

My song and praise shall be of one,
Among the greatest mortals, who,
Regarding us when struggling hard,
Quickly to our succor flew.
Undesigning in all he done,
Intrepid, wise, and generous man,
Soon for himself bright laurels won.

Disinterested, here he came,
Equipped with armor shining bright,

Leading forth his soldiers, who,
At his expense, came here to fight.
For us he fought, was wounded, too,
And for our cause did suffer pain;
Yet, soon as he recovered strength,
Enlisted in the war again.
The sun and moon will first grow dim,
The concave melt, the planets fall,
E'er men will cease to reverence him.

A Major-General in the American army; is justly celebrated for leaving an immense estate, the best of friends, and, above all, a beloved wife, to fight the battles of a strange people in a far-off country. This generous act will render his name immortal. He was born in France, September, 1757, and died at Lagrange, in 1830, and now lies buried in France, near Paris, sleeping between his heroic wife and beloved daughter.

---

### *MORAL LESSON—REASON FOR SINGULARITY.*

A CELEBRATED old General used to dress in a fantastic manner, by way of making himself better known. It is true, people would say—"Who is that old fool?" but it is also true that the answer was, "That is the famous General ———, who took such or such a place."

## ACROSTIC.

Just and holy Lamb of God!
Ever may I trust thy blood
So long as life remains to me;
Uphold me, now to thy cross I bow,
Save me by thy mercy free.

## ACROSTIC.

Leading us right, possessing might,
Our hearts and wills controlling;
Viewless, but still it seems to fill
Earth with its darts consoling.

### ACROSTIC.

Never falter, never tire,
Ever faithful horse to me;
We are traveling, traveling fastly,
Soon in sight of home to be.

---

### ACROSTIC.

Jesus Christ, the truth, the way,
On Him trust from day to day;
Harmless, blameless, strive to be,
Nor fear to own He died for thee.

---

### ACROSTIC.

We grieve that we thy scourges see,
And, supplicating, ask of thee,
Relentless monster, from us flee.

(*Composed in* 1864.)

## ACROSTIC.

Directed by wisdom,
Onward he hies,
Co-acting with men,
Those seeking a prize
Of glories now shining
Remote in the skies.

In all his acts
Such grandeur we see,
As beggars description;
A mortal more free
Can never be found,

Nor desired to be.

Concerning his goodness,
Of this we are sure,
Like a Christian he tries
Each person to cure.

---

## ACROSTIC.

May all thy days be days of bliss,
In this low world of care;
Solid and lasting peace is this
To have of death no fear.

## ACROSTIC.

Hold her canvas to the breeze,
O'er the waves she rides with ease,
Praise to God, of our life the giver,
Each one from harm he can deliver.

---

## ACROSTIC.

Most worthy and sweet,
A mirror of light;
Glittering like diamonds,
Glorious and bright;
Industrious, and giving
Each mortal delight;

Captivating our hearts,

Firm, faithful each day.
On thy name when we write,
X stands in the way.

## ACROSTIC.

Onward march, never lagging,
Never on thy riches bragging;

Let thy walls more wide extend,
And thy sons from harm defend;
Never let no foe invade thee,
Cast out those who would degrade thee;
And make thy sons and daughters be
Shining lights among the free.
Though Philadelphia is much longer,
Enriched with men, perhaps some stronger,
Regard it not, though thou art smaller.

Can she boast of houses taller?
Is she possessed of ladies fairer?
Truer? No, we can compare her,
Yea, and even prove that she

Possesses few so fair as thee;
Exquisite in their forms and features,
No city hath such lovely creatures,
Nor none possesses better preachers.
Some few on earth may be more wealthy,
Yet we know of none so healthy.
Laurels around thy walls are clinging,
Virtuous ladies, too, are singing,
And others working hard, while we
Now are speaking, praising thee.
Indeed we love no place so well,
And yet thy worth we fail to tell.

---

*VIRTUE.*

His hand the good man fastens on the skies,
And bids earth roll, nor feels her idle whirl.—Young.

## ACROSTIC.

Sweet music round this place is ringing,

Ringing softly—stop and hear;

Childs has come, just hear him singing,
He was made our hearts to cheer;
It is a piano he is playing—
Let us go and near him stand,
Detain us not, for we must buy it,
Since he keeps the best on hand.

---

## ACROSTIC.

May Heaven inspire me now with rhyme,
A power to write some pleasing line;
Rich in love, and rich in grace,
Your beauty and many charms to trace.

## ACROSTIC.

More pure than the gems of Olympian stream,
Inclining to good, of beauties the Queen;
"Seductive her charms, as a poet's young dream,"
Supremely beloved is the maid of my theme.

Many beauties I've seen, North, South, East, and West,
Acrosticised hundreds, in earnest and jest,
Respected and loved some, flattered the rest,
Yet she, and she only, reigns Queen of my breast.

High above others her accomplishments soar;
An anthem of praise might be sung of her lore,
Never written by Byron, Scott, Shakspeare, or Moore;
Nor dreamed of by poets or painters of yore!
And her wit sparkles bright amid pleasure's throng,
Heart-thrilling her accents, as love's ardent song.

Thus wisdom, and beauty, and virtue unite,
Harmonious in her as dreams of the night.
O, could I depict that transcendent delight
My heart felt when first she enraptured my sight!
All trembling with transport, I gazed on her face,
Seraphic she seemed, as an angel of grace.

---

## ACROSTIC.

(*Composed* 1860.)

Just read the name of him to be
Our President; most wise is he,
His cheerful face, as all agree,
None but his foes dislike to see.

Both parties can in him repose,
Every man, including foes;
Law-abiding man, he shows
Love for truth where'er he goes.

Born near Nashville, Tennessee, 1796, and entered public life during Federal Administration of John Quincy Adams, and in 1860 was run by the American Party as a candidate for the Presidency.

## ACROSTIC.

Clatter, clatter, here they come,
A wondrous source of power,
Running at a rapid rate,
Some thirty miles per hour.

## ACROSTIC.

All cases of headache 'twill cure at a touch,
Men and dear ladies can't praise it too much;
Because 'tis marvelous and cheering to read,
Respecting its power to cure with such speed.
Old sores, sore throats, and dyspepsia it cures,
Sprains, and all cuts, wherever it goes;
It cures the bronchitis, it cures the sore eyes,
And it cures the diarrhea, as no one denies;
Langour of spirits 'twill remove in a day,

One dose will do it—no cure no pay;
It cures all bites, for which you should buy it;
Ladies and gents afflicted now try it.

## ACROSTIC.

Enchanting men with smiles so free,
Look now on one, to love a slave;
Let me but thy admirer be,
Each day to speak in praise of thee—
No greater boon than this I crave.

For though renowned, I do not seek,
Lady, to win that heart of thine;
Of worth alone I wish to speak;
Regarding thee with pure design,
I view thee as too good and meek,
Notwithstanding sometimes I rhyme,
Ever to take this hand of mine.

But still for all, I thee admire,
On thee would gaze both day and night,
Unerring tune thy golden lyre,
Repeat those songs which give delight.
Lady, I feel a holy fire
Always when dwelling in thy sight,
Nor would I here more wealth desire,
Did I possess a gem so bright.

---

## ACROSTIC.

Blushing now with the tint of health,

Sing on God's praises free;

Bless'd with that grace, more prized than wealth,
Each sinful pleasure flee;
Looking above, and like myself,
Long with the Lord to be.

## ACROSTIC.

(*Composed in* 1860.)

Surpassed by none beneath the sun,

At his face we love to gaze;

Dull care begone, from morn till morn.
One so wise we love to praise;
Untainted by corruption's dye,
Generous man, possessing worth,
Let every State his acts relate,
And spread his fame, and him proclaim
Superior to the sons of earth.

---

### *MORAL LESSON—A WOMAN'S PROMISE.*

Henry Carey, cousin to Queen Elizabeth, after having enjoyed her majesty's favor for several years, lost it in the following manner: As he was walking one day, full of thought, in the garden of the palace, under the Queen's window, she perceived him, and said to him, in a jocular manner: "What does a man think of when he is thinking of nothing?"

"Upon a woman's promise," said Carey.

"Well done, cousin," answered Elizabeth.

She retired, but did not forget Carey's answer. Some time after he solicited the honor of a peerage, and reminded the Queen that she had promised it to him.

"True," replied she, "but that was a woman's promise."

## ACROSTIC.

Henceforth we are of him bereft,
Of him who won a name
No other mortal man has left
On these low shores of fame.
Rising from youth to fame and might,
And with the wise and great,
Benign he labored, day and night,
Long grievance to abate;
Endeared to us and deep in thought,

He did his wit display,
Even those who his ruin sought
No harm of him could say,
Refuting every doctrine bad,
Yet craving not a name;

Calm, and in his right mind clad,
Leaped up to wealth and fame.
At Washington he passed away,
Yet his fame can ne'er decay.

(*Written on his death.*)

---

## ACROSTIC.

Respected by
Each mortal true,
Victorious on

The right pursue;

Make all you can

From sin to flee;
In doing which
Now pray that we
Not one may err;
Each loving worth,
Your name revere.

## ACROSTIC.

Though tea, you know, caused blood to flow,
Extol it still, I trust you will,
And buy of me, and let me go.

---

## ACROSTIC.

All admire thy beauty, thy streets are so wide,
Undefiled by drunkards, few passing this way;
Green wave thy tall trees, of rich Georgia the pride,
Undergoing a change, for the better, each day,
Spreading and lengthening; here thousands have rolled
To greet their true friends and companions of old,
And made, by industry, ten thousands of gold.

## ACROSTIC.

Read her life, ye rich and poor,
Unbounded praises to her give;
Though she died in days of yore,
Her virtuous name will ever live.

(*The Moabitess.*)

## ACROSTIC.

Majestic and rich, her name we adore,
A comfort to all, to the rich and the poor;
Revealing true worth to the men of each State,
Yet half of her charms we can not relate;
Look at her cities and mansions around,
Alive with sweet ladies, for beauty renowned;
Neat and most lovely, behold them, we pray,
Directing their course to the mansions of day.

## ACROSTIC.

Most solemn sight, to them delight,
As their hands they willing join;
Roll on, ye years, be free from cares,
Rich flowers round their pathway twine.
It has been said that those who wed
Are the ones most free from strife;
Glad tidings to the high and low,
Each man should get a lovely wife.

### MORAL LESSON—HOW TO WIN.

A MAN who is very rich now, was very poor when he was a boy. When asked how he got his riches, he replied: "My father taught me never to play till my work was finished, never to spend money until I had earned it. If I had but half an hour's work to do in a day, I must do that the first thing, and in half an hour. And after this I was allowed to play; and I could then play with much more pleasure than if I had the thought of an unfinished task before my mind. I early formed the habit of doing every thing in its time, and it soon became perfectly easy to do so. It is to this habit I owe my prosperity."

Let every one who reads this go and do likewise, and he will meet a similar reward.

## ACROSTIC.

The learned and the wise,
How I love and I prize
Each virtue composing their worth.

Like angels they shine,
All lovely, divine,
Dispelling much darkness from earth.
In the days of their youth
Embracing the truth,
Soothing the high and the low.

Observe what I say,
For a moment, I pray,

Just view them as onward they go,
Adorning each street,
Conversing so sweet,
Kind-hearted, most noble and free,
Sublime are their ways.
On them when I gaze,
No blemish nor error I see.

---

*THE HEN AND THE SWALLOW.*

A HEN, finding some serpent's eggs in a dung-hill, sat upon them with a design to hatch them, A swallow, perceiving it, flew toward her and said, with some warmth and passion: "Are you mad, to sit hovering over a breed of such pernicious creatures as you do? Be assured, the moment you bring them to light, you are the first they will attack and wreak their venomous spite upon."

## ACROSTIC.

So lovely and sweet, with virtues complete,
And a mind unclouded and pure,
Regard what I write;
Although 'tis night,
Had I wings I'd fly to thy door.

Proud to tell, I love thee so well,

My affections are flowing to thee,
One word more, I pray—
Observe what I say,
Next week be looking for me.

---

## ACROSTIC.

Sweet smiles, more bright than rays of light,
Adorn those lovely cheeks of thine;
Looking so neat, with charms complete,
Lady, now say, wilt thou be mine?
If thou art free, by marrying me,
Each day I'll try to comfort thee,

And make thy life quite free from strife,

Justly acting toward my wife,
Expecting her my heart to cheer,
Never to scold, but call me dear.
Now hear me through, believe me, too,
I love thy smiling face to view.
No mortal man here living can
Give unto thee a heart so free,
So full of love as mine for thee.

# ORIGINAL ACROSTICS.

## ACROSTIC.

There are some who of thy future doubt;
Has thou one word? Now speak it out,
Ere thy name be lost to fame.

Already certain men are saying,
Thy vital chords they are decaying;
Lion of the sea, awake!
And make those babblers fear and quake.
Now we beseech, if thou art able,
To prove thyself a talking cable,
Interchange one word or so,
Concerning of thy present woe;

Cleave each rock beneath the sea,
And prove thyself indeed to be
Beneficial to the free;
Like a king from slumber wake,
Exulting, and thy sceptre take.

(*Composed on its refusing to operate.*)

## ACROSTIC.

Moments fast are gliding by us;
In procession on they hie,
Speechless, yet proclaiming loudly
That we are mortal, and must die;
Ere another day has fled,
Remember, sir, we may be dead.

How short our life, at longest, here;
Upon this subject let us think,
Make efforts for to win the skies,
Ere to endless pain we sink.

---

## ACROSTIC.

While now
In youth,
Love God,
Love truth;
In strength
All glorious,
March on

Victorious.

May the God
Of the free,
Overruling,
Nourish thee.

(*A boy about nine years old.*)

## ACROSTIC.

John, dear brother, onward go,
Overcoming every foe;
Heavy though thy burdens be,
Never cease to pray for me.

Look at what we have to do

Before we can bright Canaan view;
Love for God we must possess,
And pray the Lord our foes to bless;
Conscious we are born to die,
Keep thine eyes uplifted high;
With confidence to Jesus pray
Every hour throughout the day;
Loving Him who died for thee,
Let me repeat, now pray for me.

(*My youngest Brother.*)

## ACROSTIC.

Turn this book, and at us look,
Heed our features, too,
Expressive, fine, our faces shine,

To please such folks as you;
With heads but four, we want no more,
Our eyes give us no light;

Our ears are deaf, but yet no grief
Disturbs us day or night;
Deprived of feet, we can not walk
In houses where we go;
The reason why we do not sigh
Is left for you to know.
Ever free from care are we,
So turn this book, and at us look.

## ACROSTIC.

Commissioned by the king of Spain,
He did a fleet of ships prepare;
Rejoicing, westward he set sail
In search of land, he knew not where
Some asserted he would find
The ocean deep, a boundless main;
Others, by sailing west it would
Prevent his coming back again.
Hopeful still he kept his course,
Ere long our glorious land he sees,
Rich, and covered o'er with trees.

Confirmed in what he thought was true,
Our lovely land he bids farewell;
Leaving this, with joy he went
Unto his own the news to tell.
Men soon flocked here from every clime,
Both young and old, the rich and poor,
Until we see this happy land
Scattered now with cities o'er.

Christopher Columbus was a native of Genoa, and died at Valladolid, in the year 1506, being about seventy years old. But this great man was unjustly deprived of the honor of giving his name to this continent by Americus Vespucius, a native of Florence, who claimed the honor of being the first discoverer of the main land.

## ACROSTIC.

No State more free from debt than she;
O could the proud her farms but see!
Rich farms of tar, rich farms of pitch—
They would, methinks, pronounce her rich.
Her bottom-land is very good,

Covered with the best of wood,
And will produce, when cleared away,
Rich crops of wheat, rich crops of hay,
Oats, too, and corn, tobacco and rye,
Leap like tall trees, and seek the sky;
Inviting us to go and view,
Not only men, but women true,
At work in corn and cotton, too.

## ACROSTIC.

Virginia! Virginia! I love thee so well!
In youth o'er thy hills and thy streams did I roam;
Resplendent with cities, in thee could I dwell,
Glad, glad, would I leave thee, my fair sunny home.
It was on thy soil that my parents first gazed,
Near Banister river, not far from its mouth;
Industrious, their children to labor they raised,
And, hoping to enrich us, they moved to the South.

## DEAR MISS.

Thou art by far more dear to me
Than all the gold and gems that be,
Whether on land or on the sea
There's none that can compare with thee.

Thou art my own true heart's delight,
Of thee I think both day and night;
And this I deem but just and right,
Since I can live but in thy light.

## ACROSTIC.

Most lovely one,
I know of none
So learned as thee beneath the sun;
Thine eyes are bright,
Reflecting light,
Enrapturing me with true delight;
So do not scorn at me, forlorn,
Since on thy name I love to write.

Made for to cheer,
And wipe each tear
Rolling down from eyes most dear;
The humble poor
Haste to thy door,
And feed upon thy bounteous store.

Pleased with worth,
Relieving dearth.
In the highest circles on the earth,
Nymphs we see
Conversing free,
Endeavoring hard to vie with thee.

## ACROSTIC.

Neater by far than a fine gold ring,
And once on a time, hearing her sing,
Nightingales came, her presence to greet,
Conscious that they her music could beat,
Yet failing in this, did quickly retreat,

Resolving no more in the land to be heard.
Excelled at last, by a mortal endeared,
Visions of glory all vanished away;
Each fearing to speak, did secretly say
She sang more sweet than an angel to-day.

## ACROSTIC.

Fairest one, in thee we find
A virtuous, pure, contented mind;
Not only learned, not only wise;
No man of sense can fail to prize
Your captivating, lovely eyes.

Shedding light on all that be,
Making men to bow to thee;
In vain they bow, in vain they chat,
They tell thee this, they tell thee that,
Hear them not, but marry me.

(*Of Springfield, Mo.*)

## *PRAISE.*

The love of praise, howe'er concealed by art,
Reigns, more or less, and glows in every heart;
The proud, to gain it, toils on toils endure,
The modest shun it but to make it sure.—Young.

## ACROSTIC.

Boundless source of information—
Information for the blind,
Bringing words of consolation,
Life and peace to soothe the mind
Exposed to grief of every kind.

## ACROSTIC.

Newly settled,
Enriched with fountains,
Bounded by
Rough hills and mountains,
And some of them,
So very high,
Kiss every cloud
As passing by.

## ACROSTIC.

'Tis vain to try to please such folks,
Holding their heads like towering oaks;
Each wrapped in self, can plainly see

Some error in all men that be
Except themselves, in whom they view
Learning, wit, and grandeur, too.
Forgetting all but self alone,
In search of wealth; to evil prone:
Such living thus and dying so,
How can they up to glory go?

## ACROSTIC.

Enrich'd, refin'd, with brilliant mind,
Love we to sing of one so kind,
In whom we do perfection view.
Zealous in works, most learn'd and true,
Alluring to right, ye sons of might,
Behold in her all graces bright.
Enchanted by her piercing eye,
The good, the wise, the great and high,
Her name should love while ages fly.

How few on earth possess such worth,

Discreet and wise, of noble birth;
All that is true in her we view,
Made up of charms and graces, too;
Each hour, each day, she goes to pray,
Receiving strength to cheer her way;
On glory bent, with good intent
Ne'er was a soul to ruin sent.

## ACROSTIC.

While men of sense still drink of thee,
How can we hope much good to see?
It seems, indeed, most strange to me
Such men should boast as being free;
Kept in chains, in fetters bound,
Yet simple people pour thee down.

## ACROSTIC.

(*Address to Rum, Brandy, and Whisky.*)

Rivers of blood you cause to flow,
Enslaving men where'er you go;
Vain are tears of babes or wife;
Endless cares you bring, and strife;
Love and hope you banish quite.
Remorseless foes, how great your might!
In the strength of One more strong
Even than the powers of wrong,
Should we learn your sight to spurn.

## ACROSTIC.

Lovely maiden, thy charms have enraptured my gaze,
And thy various accomplishments challenge my praise.
Unlooked for, I met thee, one cold winter's night;
Refined by all graces, like an angel of light,
All thy songs and sweet smiles gave my heart true delight.

In the days of my boyhood, an angelic form
Stood by me and blessed me from evening till morn,
And thy form and thy features, thy music and lore
Beguile me, as did that bright vision of yore.
Even now, in my fancy, thy image I see,
Like a rainbow of glory bending o'er me.

Bright being of beauty, I now bow at thy shrine,
Reject not my suit, but be mine, only mine;
And strewed with sweet flowers thy pathway shall be,
Gems right from Golconda, and pearls from the sea,
Glad, glad, will I purchase and present unto thee.

---

## ACROSTIC.

Meek, modest, and kind,
And in language refined,
Respected by all, and especially by me;
Yet who could proclaim

To the world all thy charms,

Should they live while ages shall flee.
(*Of Tennessee.*)

## ACROSTIC.

That deer we see is now in danger,
Hemmed around by deadly foes;
Each one to him a total stranger,

Craves to catch him by the nose;
He seems to dread the thought of dying,
As, leaping o'er those mighty logs,
Swiftly, swiftly, now see him flying,
Ere long to be but food for dogs.

## ACROSTIC.

Seen through no glass, to the naked eye
They look like gems set in the sky;
And yet they are but planets high;
Revolving round ten thousand suns,
Swift, yet smooth, as water runs.

## ACROSTIC.

*(Composed in 1860.)*

While looking at thee such grandeur I see,
As beggars description from a mortal like me;
So enchanting thy charms, and free from alarms,
Here fain would I live secure in thine arms.
I read of thy name as connected with fame,
Not forgetting from whence thy Father he came;
Great, glorious, and free, here his image I see,
'Tis chiseled in stone, immortal to be;
On his virtues to dwell makes my bosom now swell,
Ne'er hoping, yet trying, all his merits to tell.

Could I live through all time on a subject sublime,
It would give me true joy, methinks, could I rhyme;
Though Time in its flight his image may blight,
Yet his name it will live while the stars give us light.

## ACROSTIC.

Ne'er falter nor pine, though troubles arise,
Extending, like darkness surrounding the skies,
With freedom to guide thee, till time it shall close,

Hold fast to the Union, in spite of all foes;
And the Author of freedom, the King of the skies,
Most gracious and holy, he hears all thy cries,
Protects and directs thee, unseen though he be,
Supported by him are the States of the Free;
His arms are around thee, his power defends,
Immanuel, King Jesus, the best of all friends,
Reclaim thee when swerving from truth and from right,
Ere shades of deep darkness ingulf thee in night.

## ACROSTIC.

Through thee the loveliest rivers glide,
Enriching thee on every side.
No truer hearts a State can boast,
No fairer maidens love can toast.
Each rill of thine is dear to me,
Sweet land, most lovely Tennessee.
So long as life this heart shall warm,
E'er to thee my thoughts will turn,
Emblem of the Eternal One.*

* Trinity in Unity, three States by natural division, yet one in fact.

## ACROSTIC.

*(Composed on her losing her Mother and only Daughter.)*

SWEET sister, cease to fret and pine
About departed friends of thine;
Remember now they brightly shine,
And sing of their Redeemer's love,
High in the realms of bliss above.

All their tears have ceased to flow,
No parting there, no death, no woe,
Nor chilling winds in heaven blow.

The Word of Life to them was sweet,
It led them to the Savior's feet;
They lived in peace and love with all,
So long as on this earthly ball;
We little thought their end was nigh;
Of death they speak, and without a sigh
Rejoiced that they were born to die;
They loved the Lord, and loved the day
He called them from the earth away.

*(Of Crawford County, Arkansas.)*

---

## ACROSTIC.

SOURCE of heat and source of light,
Upholding by thy strength and might
Numerous seas and planets bright.

## ACROSTIC.

Accomplished one, most kind and free,
No one on land, no one on sea,
Need ever hope to vie with thee.

How it thrills my heart to write
On one so lovely and so bright;
With a form so good and fine,
And virtues which doth sweetly shine
Resplendent as a heavenly ray
Descending from the orb of day.

(*Of Conway County, Arkansas.*)

## SYMPATHY.

Nature has cast me in so soft a mold,
That but to hear a story feigned for pleasure,
Of some sad lover's death, moistens my eyes,
And robs me of my manhood.—Dryden.

## ACROSTIC.

Go on, go on, from strength to strength,
Enterprising, and at length
One more railroad will be done,
Ready for the cars to run.
Go on, go on, improvements make,
It is time for States to wake,
And from thee some lessons take.

---

## ACROSTIC.

Country far renowned for gold,
And for soil, rich and new,
Lofty hills and torrents bold,
Immense streams, and branches, too,
Flow through thy hills of old.
O happy land, illustrious one,
Richest, brightest clime that be,
No land, no State, beneath the sun,
In all God's wide dominion free,
Acquires wealth so fast as thee.

---

## ACROSTIC.

Adorned with fields of cotton white,
Realm of wealth and realm of light,
Keeping step with States that be
Allied to all the brave and free.
New, yet firm and brave she stands,
Supporting those who till her lands;
And from men beyond the sea
She buys her coffee, spice, and tea.

## ACROSTIC.

Equaled by none of any station,
Made up of virtues shining bright;
Men of sense, of education,
Acknowledge thee a shining light.

Thou art the idol of the day,
Honored by the young and old,
One more rich, and one more gay,
My eyes did never yet behold;
And yet to think that we must part,
Sends pain and anguish to my heart.

## ACROSTIC.

Still upward gaze,
Pour forth thy praise,
Entreating God our land to save;
No one we see
Compares with thee,
Except the noble, good, and brave.
Redeemed by love,

Continue to prove,
Religion can the heart refine;
Our sins subdue,
Giving us, too,
Essential joys for which we pine.
      (*Of Memphis.*)

## ACROSTIC.

Zealous was he to keep us all free,
And to march us in triumph o'er the powers that be;
Counselor and chief in the days of our grief,
He flew to our aid, and gave us relief;
As a true worthy son, our battles he won,
Rushing on foes he made them all run,
Yelling like hounds at the crack of a gun.

The glance of his eye made the Mexicans fly,
All dreading his sword and fearing to die;
Yet thousands withstood our General so good,
Leaving his men to tread in the blood
Of cowards and foes who slept in repose,
Requiring some one their eyelids to close.

Born in Virginia, November 24, 1784. President from March 4, 1849, to his death, July 9, 1850—one year, four months and five days.

---

### *MORAL LESSON—THE TWO RIVERS.*
#### Evil communications (associations) corrupt good manners.

The waters of the Mississippi and Missouri unite and form one river. The water of the latter is exceedingly turbid, and the former clear. When they first meet the waters refuse to mingle. The clear and muddy water flows along, forming one river; but you can clearly distinguish the one from the other. By degrees the clear, bright waters of the one become united with those of the other, and the clearness is lost forever.

#### *THE APPLICATION.*

Virtuous and vicious persons can associate for a time, keeping their characters distinct. But if the associations be continued, the virtuous, pure character will become soiled by the vicious. No one can associate freely with the wicked without becoming in some measure like them.

## ACROSTIC.

Distinguished for thy skill, to save
Our fellow-men when near the grave;
Cross mighty streams thy drugs to test,
They being the purest and the best,
Of vital strength, more prized than wealth,
Restores the sick to perfect health.

Just such a man we love to view,

Learn'd in Greek and Latin, too.

Continue on thy bright career,
Our people cheering far and near,
Loving thy friends, when near the grave,
Exert thy skill each one to save.

(*My Mother's Youngest Brother, Greensboro, N. C.*)

---

## ACROSTIC.

Composed of vapors shining bright,
Of wondrous size, yet harmless light,
Men view thee as a burning ball,
Expecting soon to see thee fall
To this low world, and kill us all.

---

## ACROSTIC.

Luminous, most useful, most lovely to scan,
It falls directly or obliquely on man,
Graceful in carriage, and pleasing to behold,
Highly prized, yea, precious as gold,
The thing we most need to cheer us when old.

## ORIGINAL ACROSTICS.

### ACROSTIC.

Truly kind,
Hence we find
Each of them

Like the moon
And stars at night
Directing us
Into the right;
Each of them
Shining bright;

Offending none,
Firm and true,

Conversing free,
As ladies do;
Ne'er disposed
To act amiss;
Our good they seek,
No other bliss.

---

Unwearying in thy efforts be
To join thyself to States now free.
As happy as the sun that sheds
His rays on our devoted heads.

(*Composed on his triumphal March through Georgia.*)

Grappling with foes, he stratagem shows,
Evincing his skill wherever he goes.
Now view him, we pray, while fighting to-day,
Every one to him their homage should pay.
Rebels are lying around him, and crying
Aloud for help, while others are flying
Like Arabs, scared, pursuers defying.

So restless is he to cope with old Lee;
He's marching, and soon through Georgia will be
Extending his sway—each hour, each day—
Revealing true worth for his triumph we pray.
May the Lord's own arm protect him from harm,
And his soldiers incline to march in a line,
Never once to flag, to falter, nor pine.

Born in Lancaster, Ohio, on the 8th of February, 1820.

---

*FABLE—THE MOLE AND HER DAM.*

A young mole snuffed up her nose, and told her dam she smelt an odd kind of a smell. By and by, "O, strange! ' says she, "what a noise there is in my ears; as if ten thousand paper mills were going." A little after, she was at it again. "Look, look, what is that I see yonder? it is just like the flames of a fiery furnace." To whom the dam replied, "Prithee, child, hold your idle tongue: and if you would have us allow you any sense at all, do not affect to show more than nature has given you."

*THE APPLICATION.*

It is wonderful that affectation, that odious quality, should have been always so common and epidemical, since it is not more disagreeable to others than hurtful to the person that wears it. By affectation, we aim at being thought to possess some accomplishments which we have not, or, at showing what we have in a conceited, ostentatious manner. Now this we may be assured of, that, among discerning people at least, when we endeavor at any thing of this kind, instead of succeeding in the attempt, we detract from some real possession, and make qualities, that would otherwise pass well enough, appear nauseous and fulsome.

## ACROSTIC.

Just view the place where Jesus first
Embraced the sons of earth;
Round it he walked, and preached to men
Undying words of worth,
Salvation free to rich and poor,
And peace he came to bring;
Look now at it and Christ adore,
Ere long in it the Lord will reign
More glorious than before.

## ACROSTIC.

A business place, healthy and neat,
The point where four great railroads meet;
Laureled with cars, a good supply—
All the time those cars are rolling,
Never tiring, how consoling,
They bring us things for which we sigh,
And things we need, as none deny.

## ACROSTIC.

From what I see, some seek for thee,
As something worthy greeting;
Missing their aim, they thee proclaim
Elusive, worthless, fleeting.

## ACROSTIC.

His race is run, his work is done,
Our statesman and our friend;
No more will we his features see,
Or to his speech attend.
Rich and the poor his loss deplore,
And we that loved him well
Bewail the day he passed away,
Leaving us in tears to dwell.
Earth's fleeting breath was lost in death,

Descending to the tomb,
Around his grave bright laurels wave,
Ne'er may they cease to bloom.
In circles high death's arrows fly,
Each one bringeth sorrow;
Life's fleeting ray did pass away,

When death he hurled his arrow
Equaled by few we ever knew,
Brilliant the road he trod,
Serene in death, gave back his breath
To Christ, his mighty God.
Earth felt the blow when he sunk low;
Refulgent still his virtues glow.

(*Written on his Death.*)

## ACROSTIC.

Prized for thy worth,
Haste on thy way,
Influenced by
Love's cheering ray.

Cast all thy care
Here on the Lord,
Expecting he
Will thee reward.

## ACROSTIC.

Just here, could we all rum-shops see
At once put down, 'twould make us be
More prosperous, loving, kind, and free;
And as we do all hate to view
Immortal slain, by hundreds too;
Can we stand by and see them die,
And not against their murderers cry.

---

## ACROSTIC.

Repeat its charms, ye sons of earth,
Improving fast, possessing worth;
View all its mills and factories high,
Each looming up toward the sky;
Receive our praise, when passing by.

Here wealth is found, and not a few
Enchanting girls, and ladies too;
And all of them on whom we gaze,
Deserve from us our richest praise.

## ACROSTIC.

Very healthy, mountainous, and rich little State,
Endeared to the humble, the wise, and the great,
Restraining no one, all acting upright,
May walk from thy shores to the mansions of light.
Of all thy charms no mortal can tell,
No pen can relate them, all loving thee well,
They wish not to leave thee in far lands to dwell.

## ACROSTIC.

Dear little State, to thee we confess
Each beauty of thine we cannot express;
Language would fail us to tell of thy charms,
Adorned with fine houses, fine cities, fine farms;
With ladies most lovely, as the learned will agree,
And gentlemen from all vices quite free,
Rich and refined in the arts of true worth,
Extending thy fame to the ends of the earth.

---

In all our transactions with mankind, even in the most private and low life, we should have a special regard how, and with whom, we trust ourselves. Men, in this respect, ought to look upon each other as wolves, and to keep themselves under a secure guard, and in a continual posture of defense. Particularly upon any treaties of importance the securities on both sides should be strictly considered, and each should act with so cautious a view to their own interest as never to pledge or part with that which is the very essence and basis of their safety and well-being.

## ACROSTIC.

Discussing subjects most important, and the road before him viewing,
On his march to the battle-field, to save our glorious land from ruin,
Charming us all now looking at him, mounted on his horse so high;
The rebels they had better scatter, if they do not wish to die
On the gory field of battle, for should he meet the traitorous horde,
Rushing on them, he will slay them with his keen and glittering sword.

Just view him, with such noble soldiers, onward to Virginia going;

And a more brave and skillful leader never lived among the knowing.

Armed with silver-mounted pistols, and the strongest arm we know,
Possessing courage and skill to use it—clear the way, each rebel foe.
Please go with him to the battle-field, see him, when there, 'mid smoke and fires,
Laboring to perpetuate that freedom bought by sainted sires.
Every man should laud his bravery, conscious he is acting right;
We should follow him with gladness, and praise him, too, when we see him fight.
His arm is raised, his sword is drawn, and the rebels are falling near him,
Insurgent foes, all in the wrong, they need not hope to scare him.
Though bullets fall thick on every hand, he does not think of dying,
Exulting, see his sword now wave, while the rebels they are flying.

(*Composed on seeing him start off for the War.*)

## ACROSTIC.

CALLOUS-HEARTED, ruthless man,
He devised a wicked plan,
And took poor Lester's life away,
Regardless of the judgment-day;
Let the murderer and the knave,
Executed by the brave,
Sleep forgot within his grave.

Clothed with crimes of the blackest dye,
Observe him when he comes to die,
Supported by the sheriff's hand—
Guilty wretch, he can not stand,
Reflection seems to cast him down;
One more step, his limbs are bound
Very close, and soon he swings,
Encountering death with all its stings.

*Who was hung at Little Rock, Arkansas, 1859, for killing a man for his money.*

---

AN old writer gives the following as the amount of sleep demanded:

NATURE requires five,
 Custom gives seven,
Laziness takes nine,
 And wickedness, eleven.

## ACROSTIC.

The prettiest and the neatest, the loveliest and the sweetest,
Here I see;
Each one possessing worth, all full of life and mirth,

Laughing free
At things that please them most, and while of them I boast,
Dearest me,
I wish the world but knew how noble, wise, and true
Each seems to be,
Sent as from the skies, to make men truly wise,

And religious, too;
To soothe their hearts with joy, my pen I will employ,

Though my words be few;
How can I love them less, when they, indeed, possess
Each virtue true?

Claiming as a prize, a home beyond the skies,
Hoping for bliss,
And bidding me to follow, though I am not worth one dollar.
Let me think of this;
Yon heaven which they seek, was made for all the meek,
Beckoning me away,
Enchanting as they move, toward the place they love,
And like a ray,
They cheer me all the while, and when on me they smile,
Enriched I seem.

And for each person here, we have water good and clear,
Cooling to drink,
Increasing as it flows, a balm for earthly woes;
Do not let it sink;

So long as time shall glide, and men on earth abide,
Proclaim its worth;
Rushing from a hill, though it can not turn a mill,
It cures the sick;
No one should doubt my word, though of it they've not heard;
Gather round it quick.

## ACROSTIC.

(*Composed* 1860.)

Cement with love each State and heart,
Our Union, never let it part;
Let it, though, forever stand
Uninjured by a tyrant's hand.
Make mountains tumble in the sea,
Before we let this Union be
In its pride and glory hurled
As a wreck upon the world.

---

## ACROSTIC.

Giving lessons,
Each bright and new,
Ne'er swerving from,
Each good pursue.
Renowned for sense
And learning, too;
Lawyer, statesman,

Just, wise, and true.
A hero, brave,
Men love to view;
Each man around
Speaks well of you.

Yet life is short,
Earth's glories few,
Live not for fame
Like others do.

## ACROSTIC.

Mouldering though thy body be,
Yet in my dreams thy form I see.

My tears in torrents daily fall
O'er thee; I would, but can't recall.
Thou art gone to Christ, thy God,
He who bought thee with his blood,
Enabled thee to run thy race,
Raised thee now to see his face,

Exalted thee to hear his voice,
Lifted thee; with saints rejoice
In holy songs of perfect love—
Zion and her walls above,
And all the beauties of the skies
Before thee now in grandeur lies.
Expansive view of love divine,
Thine to view, forever thine,
Happiness without one sigh,

Precious fruits forever nigh,

Beheld by thee, by thee enjoyed,
Lasting, ne'er to be destroyed;
All thy cares and troubles o'er,
Christ thy praise for evermore.
King and Priest, be he my stay,
While here I dwell in flesh and clay,
Ever knowing death is nigh,
Let me but live, let me but die
Like thee, and meet thee in the sky.

(*Died in* 1858.)

## ACROSTIC.

My darling, I fain would cross the deep sea,
And quickly return with riches to thee;
Rubies and diamonds and pearls from the main,
Yet being so poor all my wishes are vain.
Thine eyes are stars which gladden the heart,
Bidding all gloom and sorrows depart;
Laughing and blushing, thy smiles they are balm,
And hover around my passions to calm;
Consuming their dross, and making me be
Kindly disposed, especially to thee,
With whom I do hope to spend a long life,
Exultingly, too, caressing my wife,
Laughing at want, defying all pain,
Living in hopes of living again.
        (*Composed in* 1858.)

## ACROSTIC.

*(My Wife.)*

'Mid pains and convulsions, thy soul passed away,
And rose, as I trust, to the realms of bright day;
Reviving the thought, though thy death I record,
Yet thou art now happy and praising the Lord.

To win me to Jesus thou seemed to be sent,

But, strange to relate, I refused to repent,
Loving those pleasures which last but a day;
All thy fond pleadings I threw them away,
Crushing thy hopes, and giving thee pain,
Knowing that all thy efforts were vain;
While kindness and love yet beamed in thine eyes,
Earth was exchanged for a home in the skies,
Leaving me here, without friends, without home,
Loaded with sorrows, 'mid strangers to roam.

---

But could tears of anguish wake thee
   From the dark and lonely grave,
In my arms I now would take thee,
   And bless the Lord who died to save.

But in that grave in which thou sleepeth,
   No sun on thee will ever rise;
And though thy husband o'er thee weepeth,
   Never canst thou hear his cries.

Deaf to all that now would greet thee,
   Cold thy brow and still thy heart,
Yet in heaven I hope to meet thee,
   Never more from thee to part.

*(Composed on her Death, May 23, 1859.)*

[One night, at a party, a loquacious inebriate, libertine, smoker, and chewer, asked me to write some poetry on himself and a couple of snuff-dippers who were sitting by him. The following lines I then composed, and read within their hearing:]

Some ladies do delight to joke,
    And can appreciate
The worth of those who drink and smoke,
    While sober men they hate.

They are, they think, of judges best—
    Of course it must be so;
They love the fop, and men detest
    Who can not make a show.

Go to parties where oft they meet,
    And view them all the while;
The man who talks to them most sweet,
    Though ignorant, low, and vile,

He is the man to please them most;
    While one from vices free,
Who will not drink to them a toast,
    They from his presence flee.

The time is not so distant when,
    If things go on this way,
All truly good and virtuous men
    At home had better stay,

Than to be scorned by ladies, who,
    Professing vice to hate,
Encourage drunkards not a few
    By listening to them prate.

And while some do of smoking boast,
    And love to dance and skip;

Of all the things, we hate the most
  To see one chew or dip.

And still we do regret to say,
  Some use tobacco free;
Perhaps one thousand pounds per day
  They dip in Tennessee.

Oh! what a waste of time and wealth,
  And what else does it do?
It always does impair the health,
  And kills the user, too.

'Tis dipping brings consumption on—
  This truth none can deny—
And pales the cheek, made to adorn
  The cities in the sky.

A curse on those who grind the snuff,
  Or did it first invent;
It kills its thousands; ain't this enough
  To wish it from us sent?

Had we the genius to harangue,
  We would impress on all,
That we should make a law to hang
  Snuff makers great and small.

Nor would we pass rum sellers by
  For killing mortals: we
Would make a law to hang them high
  Upon the nearest tree,

And leave them there for birds to pick—
  We mean the carrion crow—
Still some we fear it would make sick
  To feed on things so low.

## ACROSTIC.

They teach us by example bright,
Heaven-born, religious light,
Enables men to act upright.

Learned and skilled in every thing,
And when I hear them sweetly sing,
Delight doth fill my heart;
I seem as in a trance to be,
Ethereal joys encompass me;
Soon time arrives, for home I start—

One lovelier than the rest I see,
From her I would not part;

Still from her I'm forced to go,
Plodding all the country o'er,
Remembering that I am so poor
It is not wise to tarry;
Now could the lady read my heart,
Glance at it before I start,
From her I fain would never part;
I think she then would marry
Even one so poor as me.
Loveliest thing on land or sea,
Despise me not—farewell to thee.

## ACROSTIC.

Ne'er yet did mortals here on earth a purer saint behold,
Exerting all her powers to save from death the young and old;
To God, throughout the livelong day, her earnest prayers ascend;
They center round the cross of Christ, and with her father's blend.
In holy, humble converse, they about the Saviour talk;
Expounding truths, transcendent sweet, as they together walk.

Here hand in hand, with mother, too, they journey to the sky,
In search of sanctifying grace, and find a full supply
Lying within the reach of them; and on the young and hoary,
Light from above, it shone around, and filled each soul with glory.

## MISS HARRIET T.

Before we run each other down
  Let us ourselves apply,
And study truth, and cease to frown
  On mortals born to die.

The ant, you know, is very small,
  And yet it makes a hill,
Which, to it, appears as tall
  As would to us a mill.

Tne eagle, too, you will admit,
  Can soar from earth away,
But does that make it right for it
  On smaller birds to prey.

And though I never went to school
  As other folks have done,
Should you for this call me a fool,
  And at me poke your fun.

If that be right, then go ahead,
  You can not injure me;
When people try on me to tread,
  I from their presence flee;

But ere I leave, I say to you,
  Being a graduate;
And having sense to will and do,
  I must conclude, and state

It would be vain for silly men
  To cope as with an elf,
Or think of grasping wisdom, when
  You have it all yourself.

## ACROSTIC.

Ever virtuous,
Lovely, too,
In religion foremost;
Zealous and true,
Alluring to good,
Bold to defend,
Ever kind;
True to the end
Her spirit lives,

Defying death,
Ever bright
Among the saints
Now in light.

---

### GRIEF.

Like the lily,
That once was mistress of the field, and flourished,
I'll hang my head, and perish.—SHAKSPEARE.

## ACROSTIC.

(*Composed in* 1856.)

Honored for thy love of right,
Onward soar to fame and might;
Never from the truth diverging,
Or spurious doctrines on us urging;
Respect the good, reprove the bad,
And brace the weak, and cheer the sad.
Be kind to all, do what we may,
Let nothing lead thy heart astray;
Ever kind in thought and deed,

Men by acts thy heart can read.
Indebted for past favors, we,
Like loyal subjects, reverence thee.
Labor on, and be content,
And if elected President,
Restore the good to office, and
Disperse the bad, at thy command.

For many now in office be
In whom defects we plainly see;
Living on the revenue
Like wolves they eat, but nothing do.
Mean men, they seek for wealth and fame,
Our country's good is not their aim;
Repulse them all from office, and
Extend thy sway o'er all the land.

**Thirteenth President of the United States.**

Born in New York, January 7, 1800. Succeeded to the Presidency on the death of General Taylor, July 9, 1850. Served to March 4, 1853—two years, seven months and twenty-three days.

## ACROSTIC.

Make truth thy study day and night,
Impressed with subjects shining bright;
Christ, the Lord, the source of light,
Always cheering guide thee aright.
Just think upon his love so free,
All men he bids from sin to flee;
He took our place and died, that we,

Both young and old, might angels be.
Love so great was never known,
Around the earth his glories shone;
Coming from his Father's throne,
King Jesus did our sins atone.
We should not, then, forget to pray,
Exposed to death, without delay,
Let us now both in earnest say,
Lord Jesus, take our sins away.

(*My dear Brother.*)

## ACROSTIC.

Armed with all power and with love,
Look down on me from heaven above;
My only hope, my only plea,
Is that Jesus died for me.
Gracious Father, Heavenly King,
Hear me while thy praise I sing;
Though so sinful, though so vile,
Yet in mercy on me smile.

Give me grace from day to day
On Thee to trust, and when I pray
Disperse my gloomy doubts away.

## ACROSTIC.

Fam'd for wealth, for beauty and health,
Let no city outshine thyself;
Uplifted high, our wants supply,
So long as stars beam in the sky;
Here men we find for bliss designed,
Industrious, noble, wise, and kind;
Not only so, young ladies sweet,
God bless them all, they can't be beat.

## ACROSTIC.

Celebrated for industry, while factories we see
On our right and on our left when traveling o'er thee;
No one can prevent us, when on thee we gaze,
Nor make us to falter when giving thee praise.
Each one who beholds thy name should adore,
Containing the learned, the rich, and the poor;
Tall churches, large towns, and cities also,
Increasing in wealth still daily they grow.
Cheering all mortals in thy limits around,
Undeniable, most beautiful, the learned and profound,
They admit, to thy glory, thy name is renowned.

### FABLE—THE TUNNY AND THE DOLPHIN.

A fish, called a tunny, being pursued by a dolphin, and driven with great violence, not minding which way he went, was thrown by the force of the waves upon a rock, and left there. His death was now inevitable; but, casting his eye on one side, and seeing the dolphin, in the same condition, lie gasping by him, "Well," says he, "I must die, it is true; but I die with pleasure, when I behold him who is the cause of it involved in the same fate."

#### THE APPLICATION.

Revenge, though a blind, mischievous passion, is yet a very sweet thing; so sweet that it can even soothe the pangs, and reconcile us to the bitterness of death. And, indeed, it must be a temper highly philosophical that could be driven out of life by any tyrannical, unjust procedure, and not be touched with a sense of pleasure to see the author of it splitting upon the same rock.

## ACROSTIC.

Numerous mills, and factories too,
Enrich her sons and daughters true
With gold and silver bright and new.

Ye men, who buy fine goods of her,
Offend her not, her name is dear,
Reflecting light, be men profound;
Keep step with her, ye States around,

## ACROSTIC.

Prized by the good, and by the great
Enriched and called the Keystone State;
No State more true, or State more wise,
No State more loved beneath the skies;
She firmly stands, adorned with grace;
Ye men around, behold her face.
Look at her houses, white and new,
Various fine towns and cities too,
Alive with men. Now see, behold
Not only men, but women bold,
Imploring God to save our land,
And make this Union firmly stand.

### FABLE—THE ANT AND THE GRASSHOPPER.

In the winter season, a commonwealth of ants was busily employed in the management and preservation of their corn, which they exposed to the air, in heaps, round about the avenues of their little country habitation. A grasshopper, who had chanced to outlive the summer, and was ready to starve with cold and hunger, approached them with great humility, and begged that they would relieve his necessity with one grain of wheat or rye. One of the ants asked him how he had disposed of his time in summer, that he had not taken pains and laid in a stock, as they had done, "Alas! gentlemen," says he, "I passed away the time merrily and pleasantly, in drinking, singing, and dancing, and never once thought of winter." "If that be the case," replied the ant, "all I have to say is, that they who drink, sing, and dance in the summer, must starve in the winter."

*MORAL.*

Who pleasures love
Shall beggars prove.

## ACROSTIC.

Go, preach God's word, and spread it wide,
O'er earth from sea to sea;

Ye holy men, our boast and pride,
Each one must faithful be,

Insulted heaven to defend,
Not faint at heart, but strong;
Through life to preach to foe and friend,
Opposing every wrong;

And praying all from death to flee,
Loving the truth to sound;
Loudly proclaim salvation free

To dying mortals round.
High-reaching after righteousness,
Each hour watch and pray,

While traveling through this wilderness
Of doubt and care, each day,
Reveal your love for God above;
Loving to preach, poor sinners teach
Dangers thickly round them lay.

[These lines were suggested by a conversation with an individual, who requested an acrostic upon his name, who had doubts about the immortality of the soul.]

## ACROSTIC.

'Tis from the past we wisdom learn,

The future is all dark to me,
And when I to the dust return,
Where will my thinking powers be?
Will they forsake me with my breath,
Or live with God, while ages flee,
Or dwell with devils after death,
These are the thoughts that trouble me.

## ACROSTIC.

Like angels of mercy, God sent them to cheer us,
As traveling o'er earth; for when they are near us,
Depression grows lighter, while enchanted we view
In each of those ladies, patriotic and true,
Every grace and charm, which makes them appear
Shining stars of perfection, angelic and dear.

Our interest consulting, they have shown a desire
For the success of our arms, since the first gun did fire,

To put down rebellion, loud-ringing, like thunder;
Hot balls, alas! rent Sumpter asunder,
Enrapturing the South, making others to wonder.

Now see them all feeding our soldiers each day,
Organizing societies, for our triumph they pray;
Raising money so freely, to aid and to cheer us,
They study our good, all ye mortals now hear us,
How happy we feel when those ladies are near us.

[Composed in 1863.]

## ACROSTIC.

Respected by the great and high,
Be true till thou art called to die;
And in that day, come when it may,
Learned sir, to thee the Lord will say,
Dear son, arise, receive the prize !
With shouting, soar above the skies,
Immortal, free to dwell with me,
New songs to sing while ages flee.

## ACROSTIC.

See how bravely they march, with banners all flying,
Our country to save, they are fighting and dying;
Led on by brave captains, and generals most dear,
Depending on God, they have nothing to fear.
Insurgents will tremble when they see them in sight,
Each man fully equipped, and prepared for the fight;
Ragamuffins and vagrants can never once stand
So much as three fires from our chivalrous, brave band.

Others might deceive us, but in them we can trust,
For we knew they are kind, intelligent, and just.

The lovers of our homes, courageous and true,
Having pledged their honor their duty to do,
Each one is now marching with victory in view.

Not a traitor can awe defenders of truth,
Our soldiers are good, some religious from youth;
Right bravely, therefore, they can march to the field,
To teach Jeff Davis, by Jehovah revealed,
He never can make the righteous to yield.

[Composed on seeing them start off for the War.]

And now abideth FAITH, HOPE, CHARITY, these three; but the greatest of these is Charity."

A HUNTER ranging along the forest wild,
　　Saw o'er the green sward tripping,
Three maidens fair and mild,
　　Three maidens fair and mild.

Fair, queenly *Faith* came foremost,
　　Next *Love* before him passed,
With *Hope*, all bright and smiling,
　　The gayest and the last:

And said, "Now choose between us,
　　For one with thee will stay;
Choose well, or thou may'st rue it
　　When two have passed away."

He said, "All bright and lovely,
　　O why must two depart?
*Faith, Hope, Love*, stay together,
　　Possess and share my heart."

## ACROSTIC.

Rousing the wolf! Queen of the sea!
Old Ireland's sons he sought to free;
Beloved friend and martyr, he
Encounter'd foes of high degree;
Restrain'd at last, Great Britain, she,
The best of men hung on a tree.

Ere long may Ireland stronger grow—
Mow down with strength each deadly foe,
Make streams of blood from tyrants flow,
Each king behead, nor mercy show
To those who laid her son so low.

An Irish revolutionist, born in Dublin, A. D. 1780. He gained high honor at Trinity College, from which he was ultimately expelled for avowing himself a Republican. Subsequently he was arrested and tried for high treason. At his trial, he defended his own cause, addressing the judge and jury with remarkable eloquence. But in vain. He was condemned to be executed, and was hanged in the city of his birth, September 20, 1803, aged 23 years. He met his fate with courage, and won general admiration for the purity of his motives and the loftiness of his character.

www.ingramcontent.com/pod-product-compliance
Lightning Source LLC
Chambersburg PA
CBHW020148170426
43199CB00010B/936